MW01503903

Bird Watching

LOG BOOK

IF LOST RETURN TO

_____

_____

Index

Page	Date	Sightings

Page	Date	Sightings

Page	Date	Sightings

Watching Log

Location: _____

Date: _____ GPS: _____

Start time: _____ End time: _____

Weather:

Wind: _____ Temperature: _____

Sightings: _____

_____

SKETCH/PHOTO

Specie	Time	Bird behaviour	Technique

Additional notes:

Watching Log

Location: _____

Date: _____ GPS: _____

Start time: _____ End time: _____

Weather:

Wind: _____ Temperature: _____

Sightings: _____

_____

SKETCH/PHOTO

Specie	Time	Bird behaviour	Technique

Additional notes:

Watching Log

Location: _____

Date: _____ GPS: _____

Start time: _____ End time: _____

Weather: ☀ ☁ ⛅ ⛈

Wind: _____ Temperature: _____

Sightings: _____

_____

```
┌─────────────────────────────────────┐
│           SKETCH/PHOTO                │
│                                       │
│                                       │
│                                       │
│                                       │
│                                       │
│                                       │
│                                       │
│                                       │
└─────────────────────────────────────┘
```

Specie	Time	Bird behaviour	Technique

Additional notes: _____

Watching Log

Location: _____

Date: _____ GPS: _____

Start time: _____ End time: _____

Weather: ☀️ ☁️ 🌤️ 🌧️

Wind: _____ Temperature: _____

Sightings: _____

_____

_____

SKETCH/PHOTO

Specie	Time	Bird behaviour	Technique

Additional notes:

Watching Log

Location: _____

Date: _____ GPS: _____

Start time: _____ End time: _____

Weather: ☀ ☁ ⛅ 🌧

Wind: _____ Temperature: _____

Sightings: _____

_____

SKETCH/PHOTO

Specie	Time	Bird behaviour	Technique

Additional notes:

Watching Log

Location: _____

Date: _____ GPS: _____

Start time: _____ End time: _____

Weather: ☀ ☁ ⛅ 🌧

Wind: _____ Temperature: _____

Sightings: _____

_____

SKETCH/PHOTO

Specie	Time	Bird behaviour	Technique

Additional notes:

Watching Log

Location: _____

Date: _____ GPS: _____

Start time: _____ End time: _____

Weather:

Wind: _____ Temperature: _____

Sightings: _____

_____

SKETCH/PHOTO

Specie	Time	Bird behaviour	Technique

Additional notes:

Watching Log

Location:

Date: _____   GPS: _____

Start time: _____   End time: _____

Weather: ☀️   ☁️   ⛅   🌧️

Wind: _____   Temperature: _____

Sightings: _____

_____

SKETCH/PHOTO

Specie	Time	Bird behaviour	Technique

Additional notes:

Watching Log

Location: _____

Date: _____ GPS: _____

Start time: _____ End time: _____

Weather:

Wind: _____ Temperature: _____

Sightings: _____

_____

SKETCH/PHOTO

Specie	Time	Bird behaviour	Technique

Additional notes:

Watching Log

Location: _____

Date: _____ GPS: _____

Start time: _____ End time: _____

Weather: ☀ ☁ ⛅ 🌧

Wind: _____ Temperature: _____

Sightings: _____

_____

SKETCH/PHOTO

Specie	Time	Bird behaviour	Technique

Additional notes:

Watching Log

Location: _____

Date: _____ GPS: _____

Start time: _____ End time: _____

Weather: ☀ ☁ ⛅ 🌧

Wind: _____ Temperature: _____

Sightings: _____
_____

SKETCH/PHOTO

Specie	Time	Bird behaviour	Technique

Additional notes:

Watching Log

Location: _____

Date: _____ GPS: _____

Start time: _____ End time: _____

Weather: ☀ ☁ ⛅ 🌧

Wind: _____ Temperature: _____

Sightings: _____

_____

SKETCH/PHOTO

Specie	Time	Bird behaviour	Technique

Additional notes:

Watching Log

Location: _____

Date: _____ GPS: _____

Start time: _____ End time: _____

Weather:

Wind: _____ Temperature: _____

Sightings: _____

_____

SKETCH/PHOTO

Specie	Time	Bird behaviour	Technique

Additional notes:

Watching Log

Location:

Date: _____ GPS: _____

Start time: _____ End time: _____

Weather:

Wind: _____ Temperature: _____

Sightings: _____

SKETCH/PHOTO

Specie	Time	Bird behaviour	Technique

Additional notes:

Watching Log

Location: _____

Date: _____ GPS: _____

Start time: _____ End time: _____

Weather:

Wind: _____ Temperature: _____

Sightings: _____

_____

SKETCH/PHOTO

Specie	Time	Bird behaviour	Technique

Additional notes:

Watching Log

Location: _____

Date: _____ GPS: _____

Start time: _____ End time: _____

Weather:

Wind: _____ Temperature: _____

Sightings: _____

_____

SKETCH/PHOTO

Specie	Time	Bird behaviour	Technique

Additional notes:

Watching Log

Location: _____

Date: _____ GPS: _____

Start time: _____ End time: _____

Weather:

Wind: _____ Temperature: _____

Sightings: _____

_____

_____

SKETCH/PHOTO

Specie	Time	Bird behaviour	Technique

Additional notes:

Watching Log

Location: ....

Date: .... GPS: ....

Start time: .... End time: ....

Weather:

Wind: .... Temperature: ....

Sightings: ....

....

SKETCH/PHOTO

Specie	Time	Bird behaviour	Technique

Additional notes:

Watching Log

Location: _____

Date: _____ GPS: _____

Start time: _____ End time: _____

Weather:

Wind: _____ Temperature: _____

Sightings: _____

_____

SKETCH/PHOTO

Specie	Time	Bird behaviour	Technique

Additional notes:

Watching Log

Location: _____

Date: _____ GPS: _____

Start time: _____ End time: _____

Weather: ☀️ ☁️ ⛅ 🌧️

Wind: _____ Temperature: _____

Sightings: _____

_____

```
                    SKETCH/PHOTO




```

Specie	Time	Bird behaviour	Technique

Additional notes:

Watching Log

Location: _____

Date: _____ GPS: _____

Start time: _____ End time: _____

Weather:

Wind: _____ Temperature: _____

Sightings: _____

SKETCH/PHOTO

Specie	Time	Bird behaviour	Technique

Additional notes:

Watching Log

Location: _____

Date: _____ GPS: _____

Start time: _____ End time: _____

Weather:

Wind: _____ Temperature: _____

Sightings: _____
_____

SKETCH/PHOTO

Specie	Time	Bird behaviour	Technique

Additional notes:

Watching Log

Location:

Date: _____ GPS: _____

Start time: _____ End time: _____

Weather:

Wind: _____ Temperature: _____

Sightings: _____

_____

SKETCH/PHOTO

Specie	Time	Bird behaviour	Technique

Additional notes:

Watching Log

Location: _____

Date: _____ GPS: _____

Start time: _____ End time: _____

Weather:

Wind: _____ Temperature: _____

Sightings: _____

_____

SKETCH/PHOTO

Specie	Time	Bird behaviour	Technique

Additional notes:

Watching Log

Location:

Date: _____ GPS: _____

Start time: _____ End time: _____

Weather:

Wind: _____ Temperature: _____

Sightings: _____

_____

SKETCH/PHOTO

Specie	Time	Bird behaviour	Technique

Additional notes:

Watching Log

Location: _____

Date: _____ GPS: _____

Start time: _____ End time: _____

Weather: ☀ ☁ ⛅ 🌧

Wind: _____ Temperature: _____

Sightings: _____

_____

SKETCH/PHOTO

Specie	Time	Bird behaviour	Technique

Additional notes: _____

_____

_____

_____

Watching Log

Location: _____

Date: _____ GPS: _____

Start time: _____ End time: _____

Weather:

Wind: _____ Temperature: _____

Sightings: _____

_____

SKETCH/PHOTO

Specie	Time	Bird behaviour	Technique

Additional notes:

Watching Log

Location: ....

Date: .... GPS: ....

Start time: .... End time: ....

Weather:

Wind: .... Temperature: ....

Sightings: ....

....

SKETCH/PHOTO

Specie	Time	Bird behaviour	Technique

Additional notes:

Watching Log

Location:

Date: _____ GPS: _____

Start time: _____ End time: _____

Weather:

Wind: _____ Temperature: _____

Sightings: _____

_____

SKETCH/PHOTO

Specie	Time	Bird behaviour	Technique

Additional notes:

Watching Log

Location:

Date: _____ GPS: _____

Start time: _____ End time: _____

Weather:

Wind: _____ Temperature: _____

Sightings: _____

SKETCH/PHOTO

Specie	Time	Bird behaviour	Technique

Additional notes:

Watching Log

Location: _____

Date: _____ GPS: _____

Start time: _____ End time: _____

Weather: ☀️ ☁️ ⛅ 🌧️

Wind: _____ Temperature: _____

Sightings: _____

_____

SKETCH/PHOTO

Specie	Time	Bird behaviour	Technique

Additional notes: _____

_____

_____

_____

_____

Watching Log

Location:

Date: _____ GPS: _____

Start time: _____ End time: _____

Weather:

Wind: _____ Temperature: _____

Sightings: _____

SKETCH/PHOTO

Specie	Time	Bird behaviour	Technique

Additional notes:

Watching Log

Location: _____

Date: _____ GPS: _____

Start time: _____ End time: _____

Weather: ☀️ ☁️ 🌤️ 🌧️

Wind: _____ Temperature: _____

Sightings: _____

_____

```
                    SKETCH/PHOTO




```

Specie	Time	Bird behaviour	Technique

Additional notes:

Watching Log

Location: _____

Date: _____ GPS: _____

Start time: _____ End time: _____

Weather:

Wind: _____ Temperature: _____

Sightings: _____

_____

SKETCH/PHOTO

Specie	Time	Bird behaviour	Technique

Additional notes:

Watching Log

Location: _____

Date: _____ GPS: _____

Start time: _____ End time: _____

Weather: ☀ ☁ ⛅ 🌧

Wind: _____ Temperature: _____

Sightings: _____

_____

SKETCH/PHOTO

Specie	Time	Bird behaviour	Technique

Additional notes:

Watching Log

Location: ....

Date: .... GPS: ....

Start time: .... End time: ....

Weather:

Wind: .... Temperature: ....

Sightings: ....

....

SKETCH/PHOTO

Specie	Time	Bird behaviour	Technique

Additional notes:

Watching Log

Location: _____

Date: _____ GPS: _____

Start time: _____ End time: _____

Weather: ☀️ ☁️ ⛅ 🌧️

Wind: _____ Temperature: _____

Sightings: _____

_____

SKETCH/PHOTO

Specie	Time	Bird behaviour	Technique

Additional notes:

Watching Log

Location: _____

Date: _____ GPS: _____

Start time: _____ End time: _____

Weather:

Wind: _____ Temperature: _____

Sightings: _____

_____

SKETCH/PHOTO

Specie	Time	Bird behaviour	Technique

Additional notes: _____

_____

_____

_____

_____

Watching Log

Location: _____

Date: _____ GPS: _____

Start time: _____ End time: _____

Weather:

Wind: _____ Temperature: _____

Sightings: _____

_____

SKETCH/PHOTO

Specie	Time	Bird behaviour	Technique

Additional notes:

Watching Log

Location:

Date: _____ GPS: _____

Start time: _____ End time: _____

Weather:

Wind: _____ Temperature: _____

Sightings:

SKETCH/PHOTO

Specie	Time	Bird behaviour	Technique

Additional notes:

Watching Log

Location:

Date: _____ GPS: _____

Start time: _____ End time: _____

Weather:

Wind: _____ Temperature: _____

Sightings: _____

SKETCH/PHOTO

Specie	Time	Bird behaviour	Technique

Additional notes: _____

_____

_____

_____

_____

Watching Log

Location: _____

Date: _____ GPS: _____

Start time: _____ End time: _____

Weather: ☀ ☁ ⛅ 🌧

Wind: _____ Temperature: _____

Sightings: _____

_____

```
                    SKETCH/PHOTO



```

Specie	Time	Bird behaviour	Technique

Additional notes:

Watching Log

Location:

Date: _____ GPS: _____

Start time: _____ End time: _____

Weather:

Wind: _____ Temperature: _____

Sightings:

SKETCH/PHOTO

Specie	Time	Bird behaviour	Technique

Additional notes:

Watching Log

Location: _____

Date: _____ GPS: _____

Start time: _____ End time: _____

Weather:

Wind: _____ Temperature: _____

Sightings: _____

SKETCH/PHOTO

Specie	Time	Bird behaviour	Technique

Additional notes:

Watching Log

Location: _____

Date: _____ GPS: _____

Start time: _____ End time: _____

Weather:

Wind: _____ Temperature: _____

Sightings: _____

_____

SKETCH/PHOTO

Specie	Time	Bird behaviour	Technique

Additional notes:

Watching Log

Location: _____

Date: _____ GPS: _____

Start time: _____ End time: _____

Weather:

Wind: _____ Temperature: _____

Sightings: _____

_____

SKETCH/PHOTO

Specie	Time	Bird behaviour	Technique

Additional notes:

Watching Log

Location: _____

Date: _____ GPS: _____

Start time: _____ End time: _____

Weather: ☀️ ☁️ 🌤️ 🌧️

Wind: _____ Temperature: _____

Sightings: _____

_____

SKETCH/PHOTO

Specie	Time	Bird behaviour	Technique

Additional notes:

Watching Log

Location: _____

Date: _____ GPS: _____

Start time: _____ End time: _____

Weather: ☀ ☁ ⛅ 🌧

Wind: _____ Temperature: _____

Sightings: _____

_____

┌───┐
│   │
│   SKETCH/PHOTO   │
│   │
│   │
│   │
│   │
│   │
│   │
│   │
│   │
│   │
└───┘

Specie	Time	Bird behaviour	Technique

Additional notes:

Watching Log

Location: _____

Date: _____ GPS: _____

Start time: _____ End time: _____

Weather:

Wind: _____ Temperature: _____

Sightings: _____

_____

SKETCH/PHOTO

Specie	Time	Bird behaviour	Technique

Additional notes:

Watching Log

Location:

Date: GPS:

Start time: End time:

Weather:

Wind: Temperature:

Sightings:

SKETCH/PHOTO

Specie	Time	Bird behaviour	Technique

Additional notes:

Watching Log

Location: ....

Date: .... GPS: ....

Start time: .... End time: ....

Weather:

Wind: .... Temperature: ....

Sightings: ....

SKETCH/PHOTO

Specie	Time	Bird behaviour	Technique

Additional notes:

Watching Log

Location: _____

Date: _____ GPS: _____

Start time: _____ End time: _____

Weather:

Wind: _____ Temperature: _____

Sightings: _____

_____

SKETCH/PHOTO

Specie	Time	Bird behaviour	Technique

Additional notes:

Watching Log

Location: _____

Date: _____   GPS: _____

Start time: _____   End time: _____

Weather:

Wind: _____   Temperature: _____

Sightings: _____

_____

SKETCH/PHOTO

Specie	Time	Bird behaviour	Technique

Additional notes:

Watching Log

Location: _____

Date: _____ GPS: _____

Start time: _____ End time: _____

Weather:

Wind: _____ Temperature: _____

Sightings: _____

_____

SKETCH/PHOTO

Specie	Time	Bird behaviour	Technique

Additional notes:

Watching Log

Location:

Date: GPS:

Start time: End time:

Weather:

Wind: Temperature:

Sightings:

SKETCH/PHOTO

Specie	Time	Bird behaviour	Technique

Additional notes:

Watching Log

Location: _____

Date: _____ GPS: _____

Start time: _____ End time: _____

Weather: ☀ ☁ ⛅ 🌧

Wind: _____ Temperature: _____

Sightings: _____

_____

SKETCH/PHOTO

Specie	Time	Bird behaviour	Technique

Additional notes:

Watching Log

Location: _____

Date: _____ GPS: _____

Start time: _____ End time: _____

Weather:

Wind: _____ Temperature: _____

Sightings: _____

_____

SKETCH/PHOTO

Specie	Time	Bird behaviour	Technique

Additional notes: _____

Watching Log

Location: _____

Date: _____ GPS: _____

Start time: _____ End time: _____

Weather: ☀ ☁ ⛅ 🌧

Wind: _____ Temperature: _____

Sightings: _____

_____

SKETCH/PHOTO

Specie	Time	Bird behaviour	Technique

Additional notes:

Watching Log

Location: _____

Date: _____ GPS: _____

Start time: _____ End time: _____

Weather: ☀ ☁ ⛅ 🌧

Wind: _____ Temperature: _____

Sightings: _____

_____

_____

SKETCH/PHOTO

Specie	Time	Bird behaviour	Technique

Additional notes:

Watching Log

Location: ....

Date: .... GPS: ....

Start time: .... End time: ....

Weather:

Wind: _____ Temperature: _____

Sightings: ....

....

```
SKETCH/PHOTO
```

Specie	Time	Bird behaviour	Technique

Additional notes:

Made in the USA
Monee, IL
12 March 2020

23070385R00074